THE ILLUSTRATED
Edgar Allan Poe

25 ESSENTIAL POEMS

EDITED BY
RYAN G.
VAN CLEAVE

MOON
SHOWER

MOON
SHOWER

Introduction and supplemental material © 2023 by Ryan G. Van Cleave

Published by Moonshower, an imprint of Bushel & Peck Books.
All rights reserved. No part of this publication may be reproduced
without written permission from the publisher.

Bushel & Peck Books is a family-run publishing house based in Fresno,
California, that believes in uplifting children with the highest standards of
art, music, literature, and ideas. Find beautiful books for gifted
young minds at www.bushelandpeckbooks.com.

Our family is dedicated to fighting illiteracy all over the world. For every book
we sell, we donate one to a child in need——book for book. To nominate a
school or organization to receive free books, please visit
www.bushelandpeckbooks.com.

Design and illustration by David Miles.
Type set in Baskerville and Calder.
Collage illustrations were created digitally from various public domain
works and/or elements licensed from Shutterstock.com.

LCCN: 2022948929
ISBN: 9781638191469

First Edition

Printed in China

10 9 8 7 6 5 4 3 2 1

Selections

LOVE & LONGING

THE GREAT BEYOND

THE WORLD FANTASTIC

INTRODUCTION

Welcome to the Illustrated Poets series! Here are three suggestions to help you make the most of this book.

SUGGESTION 1: Enjoy the poems. This seems far more important than trying to puzzle out what the author meant (or what other people believe the author meant).

SUGGESTION 2: Engage with the poems by asking questions. Here are three that should prove useful for any poem you encounter:

- *What do you notice about this poem?*

- *How does this poem make you feel?*

- *What else have you read/seen/experienced that connects with this poem?*

You'll also find individual questions suggested for each poem in this book.

SUGGESTION 3: Be your own boss. Read the poems in order or jump around as you see fit. Share them or savor them all by yourself. Say them aloud or whisper their words in your heart.

Poetry makes life better. There is NO wrong way to experience a poem.

So, read on, dear friend. And thank you for choosing poetry.

Ryan G. Van Cleave
Series Editor

PART I

Love & Longing

TO ZANTE

Fair isle, that from the fairest of all flowers,
    Thy gentlest of all gentle names **dost** take!
How many memories of what radiant hours
    At sight of thee and thine at once awake!
How many scenes of what departed bliss!
    How many thoughts of what entombed hopes!
How many visions of a maiden that is
    No more—no more upon thy **verdant** slopes!
No more! alas, that magical sad sound
    Transforming all! Thy charms shall please no more—
Thy memory *no more*! Accursed ground
    Henceforth I hold thy flower-enamelled shore,
O **hyacinthine** isle! O purple Zante!
    "Isola d'oro! Fior di Levante!"

Where do you notice repetition most in this poem?

What effect does having so many exclamation points create?

In what way is this island "accursed ground"?

IMAGINE

If this island could speak, what would it say in response to this poem?

DEFINE

Zante: *Greek island*

dost: *do*

verdant: *rich with vegetation*

hyacinthine: *covered in hyacinth flowers*

Isola d'oro! Fior di Levante!: *Island of Gold! Flower of the Levant! (Italian)*

ALONE

From childhood's hour I have not been
As others were—I have not seen
As others saw—I could not bring
My passions from a common spring—
From the same source I have not taken
My sorrow—I could not awaken
My heart to joy at the same tone—
And all I lov'd—*I* lov'd alone—
Then—in my childhood—in the dawn
Of a most stormy life—was drawn

From ev'ry depth of good and ill
The mystery which binds me still—
From the **torrent**, or the fountain—
From the red cliff of the mountain—
From the sun that 'round me roll'd
In its autumn **tint** of gold—
From the lightning in the sky
As it pass'd me flying by—
From the thunder, and the storm—
And the cloud that took the form
(When the rest of Heaven was blue)
Of a demon in my view—

ENGAGE

What might be "the mystery which binds me still"?

What emotions are created by the specific colors in this poem?

Why might a poem end with a dash instead of other punctuation?

IMAGINE

If this poem were planted in a garden, what kind of nourishment would it need to grow? What would eventually sprout from it?

DEFINE

torrent: *flood of water*

tint: *shade of a color*

A VALENTINE

For her these lines are penned, whose **luminous** eyes,
Bright and expressive as the stars of **Leda**,
Shall find her own sweet name that, nestling, lies
Upon this page, enwrapped from every reader.
Search narrowly these words, which hold a treasure
Divine—a **talisman**—an amulet
That must be worn *at heart*. Search well the measure—
The words—the letters themselves. Do not forget
The smallest point, or you may lose your labor.
And yet there is in this no **Gordian knot**,
Which one might not undo without a **sabre**
If one could merely understand the plot.
Upon the open page on which are peering
Such sweet eyes now, there lies, I say, **perdu**,
A musical name, oft uttered in the hearing
Of poets, by poets—for the name is a poet's too.
In common sequence set, the letters lying,
Compose a sound delighting all to hear—
Ah, this you'd have no trouble in **descrying**
Were you not something, of a **dunce**, my dear—
And now I leave these riddles to their **Seer**.

ENGAGE

Why do you think the speaker hides the intended recipient of this valentine poem?

Where do you most notice this poem's rhythm? How would you describe it?

Can this be both a good puzzle and a good poem? (Refer to the back matter for the solution to the puzzle here, if needed!)

IMAGINE

Answer these three Gs: What's Good about this poem? What's Goofy about it? What Goal does it try to achieve?

DEFINE

luminous: *full of light*

Leda: *Spartan queen*

talisman: *object of protection or luck*

Gordian knot: *extremely difficult problem*

sabre: *curved sword*

perdu: *hidden or concealed*

descrying: *catch sight of*

dunce: *foolish person*

Seer: *witness*

TO HELEN

Helen, thy beauty is to me
    Like those **Nicéan barks of yore**,
That gently, o'er a perfumed sea,
    The weary, way-worn wanderer bore
    To his own native shore.

On desperate seas long **wont** to roam,
    Thy **hyacinth** hair, thy classic face,
Thy **Naiad** airs have brought me home
    To the glory that was Greece
And the grandeur that was Rome.

Lo! in yon brilliant window-niche
    How statue-like I see thee stand,
    The **agate** lamp within thy hand!
Ah, **Psyche**, from the regions which
    Are Holy-Land!

ENGAGE

How might a "weary, way-worn wanderer" feel when returning to their "native shore"?

Why does Helen seem so important? What does she represent to the speaker?

Why does the speaker switch to addressing Psyche at the end?

IMAGINE

For no more than three minutes, research Helen of Troy. How does that new information affect how you read this poem?

DEFINE

Nicéan barks of yore: *ancient Greek ships*

wont: *accustomed*

hyacinth: *flower with curly petals*

Naiad: *water spirit*

agate: *shiny ornamental stone*

Psyche: *Greek goddess of the soul*

TO M—

1

O! I care not that my earthly lot
  Hath—little of Earth in it—
That years of love have been forgot
  In the fever of a minute—

2

I heed not that the **desolate**
  Are happier, sweet, than I—
But that you meddle with my fate
  Who am a passer-by.

3

It is not that my **founts** of bliss
    Are gushing—strange! with tears—
Or that the thrill of a single kiss
    Hath **palsied** many years—

4

'Tis not that the flowers of **twenty springs**
    Which have wither'd as they rose
Lie dead on my heart-strings
    With the weight of an age of snows.

5

Not that the grass—O! may it thrive!
    On my grave is growing or grown—
But that, while I am dead yet alive
    I cannot be, lady, alone.

ENGAGE

In earlier versions of this poem, the title was "Alone." Which title do you prefer?

Does it seem like the speaker knows this lady well, or is this admiration from a distance?

How might the speaker be both "dead yet alive"?

IMAGINE

If this poem had a sixth stanza, where would it fit in the poem? What would it say?

DEFINE

desolate: *lonely people*

founts: *fountains*

palsied: *having involuntary tremors*

twenty springs: *Edgar was 20 years old when this poem was written*

THE HAPPIEST DAY

The happiest day—the happiest hour
  My **sear'd and blighted** heart **hath** known,
The highest hope of pride and power,
  I feel hath flown.

Of power! said I? Yes! such **I ween**
  But they have vanish'd long, alas!
The visions of my youth have been—
  But let them pass.

And, pride, what have I now with thee?
  Another brow may ev'n inherit
The venom thou hast pour'd on me
  Be still, my spirit!

The happiest day—the happiest hour
  Mine eyes shall see—have ever seen,
The brightest glance of pride and power,
  I feel—have been:

But were that hope of pride and power
  Now offer'd with the pain
Ev'n *then* I felt—that brightest hour
  I would not live again:

For on its wing was dark **alloy**,
  And as it flutter'd—fell
An essence—powerful to destroy
  A soul that knew it well.

ENGAGE

Why is the speaker convinced their happiest day is in the past?

What kind of venom does pride have?

In what way might this be a poem about poetry?

IMAGINE

If this poem had a secret nickname, what would it be? Would the poem like that nickname better than its title?

DEFINE

sear'd and blighted: *burned and shriveled*

hath: *has*

ween: *suppose*

alloy: *metal*

Thank Heaven! the crisis—
  The danger, is past,
And the lingering illness
  Is over at last—
And the fever called "Living"
  Is conquered at last.

Sadly, I know
  I am **shorn** of my strength,
And no muscle I move
  As I lie at full length—
But no matter!—I feel
  I am better at length.

And I rest so composedly,
  Now, in my bed,
That any beholder
  Might fancy me dead—
Might start at beholding me,
  Thinking me dead.

The moaning and groaning,
  The sighing and sobbing,
Are quieted now,
  With that horrible throbbing
At heart:—ah, that horrible,
  Horrible throbbing!

The sickness—the nausea—
  The pitiless pain—
Have ceased, with the fever
  That maddened my brain—
With the fever called "Living"
  That burned in my brain.

And oh! of all tortures
　　That torture the worst
Has **abated**—the terrible
　　Torture of thirst
For the **napthaline** river
　　Of Passion **accurst**:—
I have drank of a water
　　That quenches all thirst:—

Of a water that flows,
　　With a lullaby sound,
From a spring but a very few
　　Feet under ground—
From a cavern not very far
　　Down under ground.

And ah! let it never
　　Be foolishly said
That my room it is gloomy
　　And narrow my bed;
For man never slept
　　In a different bed—
And, to *sleep*, you must slumber
　　In just such a bed.

My **tantalized** spirit
　　Here blandly reposes,
Forgetting, or never
　　Regretting its roses—
Its old **agitations**
　　Of myrtles and roses:

For now, while so quietly
　　Lying, it fancies
A holier odor
　　About it, of **pansies**—
A rosemary odor,
　　Commingled with pansies—
With **rue** and the beautiful
　　Puritan pansies.

And so it lies happily,
　　Bathing in many
A dream of the truth
　　And the beauty of Annie—
Drowned in a bath
　　Of the **tresses** of Annie.

She tenderly kissed me,
　　She fondly caressed,
And then I fell gently
　　To sleep on her breast—
Deeply to sleep
　　From the heaven of her breast.

When the light was extinguished,
　　She covered me warm,
And she prayed to the angels
　　To keep me from harm—
To the queen of the angels
　　To shield me from harm.

And I lie so composedly,
　　Now, in my bed,
(Knowing her love)
　　That you fancy me dead—
And I rest so contentedly,
　　Now in my bed
(With her love at my breast).
　　That you fancy me dead—
That you shudder to look at me,
　　Thinking me dead:—

But my heart it is brighter
　　Than all of the many
Stars in the sky,
　　For it sparkles with Annie—
It glows with the light
　　Of the love of my Annie—
With the thought of the light
　　Of the eyes of my Annie.

TO ONE IN PARADISE

Thou wast that all to me, love,
　　For which my soul did **pine**—
A green isle in the sea, love,
　　A fountain and a shrine,
All wreathed with fairy fruits and flowers,
　　And all the flowers were mine.

Ah, dream too bright to last!
　　Ah, starry Hope! that didst arise
But to be overcast!
　　A voice from out the Future cries,
"On! on!"—but o'er the Past
　　(Dim gulf!) my spirit hovering lies
Mute, motionless, aghast!

For, alas! alas! with me
　　The light of Life is o'er!
No more—no more—no more—
　　(Such language holds the solemn sea
To the sands upon the shore)
　　Shall bloom the thunder-blasted tree,
Or the stricken eagle soar!

And all my days are trances,
　　And all my nightly dreams
Are where thy grey eye glances,
　　And where thy footstep gleams—
In what **ethereal** dances,
　　By what eternal streams.

ENGAGE

Why might the speaker emphasize that "all the flowers were mine"?

When reading this poem aloud, how does it feel to repeat "no more"?

If "thunder-blasted trees" or "stricken eagles" recover, will they ever be the same?

IMAGINE

If you were going to create a video to accompany this poem, what are some things you might include?

DEFINE

pine: *yearn for*

ethereal: *light and delicate*

21

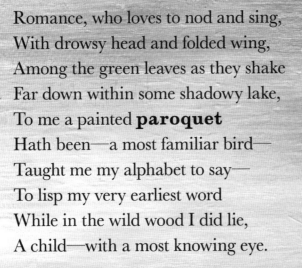

ROMANCE

Romance, who loves to nod and sing,
With drowsy head and folded wing,
Among the green leaves as they shake
Far down within some shadowy lake,
To me a painted **paroquet**
Hath been—a most familiar bird—
Taught me my alphabet to say—
To lisp my very earliest word
While in the wild wood I did lie,
A child—with a most knowing eye.

Of late, eternal **Condor** years
So shake the very Heaven on high
With **tumult** as they thunder by,
I have no time for idle cares
Through gazing on the unquiet sky.
And when an hour with calmer wings
Its down upon my spirit flings—
That little time with **lyre** and rhyme
To while away—forbidden things!
My heart would feel to be a crime
Unless it trembled with the strings.

ENGAGE

Is it important that
the speaker sees the
bird's reflection in the
lake instead of seeing
the bird directly?

What is the "most
knowing eye" of a
child?

Why are "time with
lyre and rhyme"
"forbidden things" for
this speaker?

IMAGINE

Using straws,
cardboard, paper
towel rolls, pipe
cleaners, or clay,
make a visual
representation of this
poem.

DEFINE

paroquet: *long-tailed tropical parrot*

Condor: *largest bird of prey*

tumult: *disturbance*

lyre: *small harp*

PART II

The Great Beyond

THE CONQUEROR WORM

Lo! 'tis a gala night
    Within the lonesome latter years!
An angel **throng**, **bewinged**, **bedight**
    In veils, and drowned in tears,
Sit in a theatre, to see
    A play of hopes and fears,
While the orchestra breathes fitfully
    The **music of the spheres**.

Mimes, in the form of God on high,
    Mutter and mumble low,
And **hither and thither** fly—
    Mere puppets they, who come and go
At bidding of vast formless things
    That shift the scenery to and fro,
Flapping from out their **Condor** wings
    Invisible **Wo**!

That **motley** drama—oh, be sure
    It shall not be forgot!
With its Phantom chased for evermore,
    By a crowd that seize it not,
Through a circle that ever returneth in
    To the self-same spot,
And much of Madness, and more of Sin,
    And Horror the soul of the plot.

But see, amid the mimic rout
    A crawling shape intrude!
A blood-red thing that writhes from out
    The scenic solitude!
It writhes!—it writhes!—with mortal pangs
    The mimes become its food,
And **seraphs** sob at vermin fangs
    In human gore **imbued**.

Out—out are the lights—out all!
　　And, over each quivering form,
The curtain, a funeral **pall**,
　　Comes down with the rush of a storm,
While the angels, all **pallid** and **wan**,
　　Uprising, unveiling, affirm
That the play is the tragedy, "Man,"
　　And its hero the Conqueror Worm.

ENGAGE

Why do you think the "angel throng" watches the play?

What do you notice most about the play itself?

Is the Conqueror Worm the real hero in this play?

IMAGINE

Invent a Poe-like superhero who can battle the Conqueror Worm. What's that hero's name? What do they look/dress like? What powers do they have?

DEFINE

throng: *crowd*

bewinged: *having wings*

bedight: *dressed*

music of the spheres: *imagined harmonious sound of celestial bodies moving*

Mimes: *silent comic performers*

hither and thither: *in various directions*

Condor: *largest bird of prey*

Wo: *woe*

motley: *colorful*

seraphs: *highest order of angels*

imbued: *filled*

pall: *coffin covering*

pallid: *pale*

wan: *strained*

THE CITY IN THE SEA

Lo! Death has reared himself a throne
In a strange city lying alone
Far down within the dim West,
Where the good and the bad and the worst and the best
Have gone to their eternal rest.
There shrines and palaces and towers
(Time-eaten towers that tremble not!)
Resemble nothing that is ours.
Around, by lifting winds forgot,
Resignedly beneath the sky
The melancholy waters lie.

No rays from the holy heaven come down
On the long night-time of that town;
But light from out the **lurid** sea
Streams up the turrets silently—
Gleams up the pinnacles far and free
Up domes—up spires—up kingly halls—
Up **fanes**—up **Babylon**-like walls—
Up shadowy long-forgotten bowers
Of sculptured ivy and stone flowers—
Up many and many a marvellous shrine
Whose wreathed **friezes** intertwine
The **viol**, the violet, and the vine.

Resignedly beneath the sky
The melancholy waters lie.
So blend the **turrets** and shadows there
That all seem **pendulous** in air,
While from a proud tower in the town
Death looks gigantically down.

There open fanes and gaping graves
Yawn level with the **luminous** waves;
But not the riches there that lie
In each idol's diamond eye—
Not the gaily-jewelled dead
Tempt the waters from their bed;
For no ripples curl, alas!
Along that wilderness of glass—
No swellings tell that winds may be
Upon some far-off happier sea—
No heavings hint that winds have been
On seas less hideously serene.

But lo, a stir is in the air!
The wave—there is a movement there!
As if the towers had thrust aside,
In slightly sinking, the dull tide—
As if their tops had feebly given
A void within the filmy Heaven.
The waves have now a redder glow—
The hours are breathing faint and low—
And when, amid no earthly moans,
Down, down that town shall settle hence,
Hell, rising from a thousand thrones,
Shall do it **reverence**.

ENGAGE

Earlier versions of this poem had other titles: "The City of Sin" and "The Doomed City." Which title do you like most?

Is anybody going to miss this city when it's gone?

What might this doomed city be a symbol for?

IMAGINE

If you were asked to compare this poem to a book, film, or TV show, which would you choose and why?

DEFINE

Resignedly: *accepting something unpleasant*

lurid: *fierce*

fanes: *shrines*

Babylon: *ancient city of sin and corruption*

friezes: *decoration along the top of walls*

viol: *six-stringed instrument, larger than a violin*

turrets: *small towers*

pendulous: *loosely hanging*

luminous: *full of light*

reverence: *deep respect*

THE VALLEY OF UNREST

Once it smiled a silent **dell**
Where the people did not dwell;
They had gone unto the wars,
Trusting to the mild-eyed stars,
Nightly, from their **azure** towers,
To keep watch above the flowers,
In the midst of which all day
The red sun-light lazily lay.
Now each visitor shall confess
The sad valley's restlessness.
Nothing there is motionless.
Nothing save the airs that brood
Over the magic solitude.
Ah, by no wind are stirred those trees
That **palpitate** like the chill seas
Around the misty **Hebrides**!
Ah, by no wind those clouds are driven
That rustle through the unquiet Heaven
Uneasily, from **morn till even**,
Over the violets there that lie
In **myriad** types of the human eye—
Over the lilies there that wave
And weep above a nameless grave!
They wave:—from out their fragrant tops
Eternal dews come down in drops.
They weep:—from off their delicate stems
Perennial tears descend in gems.

ENGAGE

Why might this valley have gone from smiles to sadness and restlessness?

Heaven is "unquiet." Why do you think that's the case?

Lilies are symbols of love, purity, and resurrection. How does that inform your reading of the ending?

IMAGINE

Create a four-panel comic of this poem. Use speech bubbles with invented dialogue, as needed.

DEFINE

dell: *small valley*

azure: *sky blue*

palpitate: *tremble*

Hebrides: *group of rocky Scottish islands*

morn till even: *morning until night*

myriad: *countless*

Perennial: *continually recurring*

SPIRITS OF THE DEAD

I

Thy soul shall find itself alone
'Mid dark thoughts of the gray tomb-stone—
Not one, of all the crowd, to pry
Into thine hour of secrecy:

II

Be silent in that solitude
    Which is not loneliness—for then
The spirits of the dead who stood
    In life before thee are again
In death around thee—and their will
Shall then overshadow thee: be still.

III

The night—tho' clear—shall frown—
And the stars shall look not down,
From their high thrones in the heaven,
With light like Hope to mortals given—
But their red orbs, without beam,
To thy weariness shall seem
As a burning and a fever
Which would cling to thee for ever:

IV

Now are thoughts thou shalt not banish—
Now are visions **ne'er** to vanish—
From thy spirit shall they pass
No more—like dew-drop from the grass.

V

The breeze—the breath of God—is still—
And the mist upon the hill
Shadowy—shadowy—yet unbroken,
Is a symbol and a token—
How it hangs upon the trees,
A mystery of mysteries!—

ENGAGE

Are these spirits frightening? Friendly? How does the speaker want you to engage with them?

Is Hope presented as a positive thing in this poem?

What do you think "mist upon the hill" might represent?

IMAGINE

Rearrange the stanzas as you see fit. How does the poem read differently? Does the meaning change?

DEFINE

ne'er: *never*

ANNABEL LEE

It was many and many a year ago,
    In a kingdom by the sea,
That a maiden there lived whom you may know
    By the name of Annabel Lee;—
And this maiden she lived with no other thought
    Than to love and be loved by me.

I was a child and *she* was a child,
    In this kingdom by the sea,
But we loved with a love that was more than love—
    I and my Annabel Lee—
With a love that the winged **seraphs** of Heaven
    Coveted her and me.

And this was the reason that, long ago,
    In this kingdom by the sea,
A wind blew out of a cloud by night, chilling
    My beautiful Annabel Lee;
So that her high-born kinsman came
    And bore her away from me,
To shut her up in a **sepulchre**
    In this kingdom by the sea.

The angels, not half so happy in Heaven,
    Went envying her and me
Yes!—that was the reason (as all men know,
    In this kingdom by the sea)
That the wind came out of a cloud by night,
    Chilling and killing my Annabel Lee.

But our love it was stronger by far than the love
    Of those who were older than we—
    Of many far wiser than we—
And neither the angels in Heaven above,
    Nor the demons down under the sea,
Can ever **dissever** my soul from the soul
    Of the beautiful Annabel Lee:—

For the moon never beams without bringing me dreams
    Of the beautiful Annabel Lee;
And the stars never rise, but I feel the bright eyes
    Of the beautiful Annabel Lee:—
And so, all the night-tide, I lie down by the side
Of my darling—my darling—my life and my bride,
    In her sepulchre there by the sea—
    In her tomb by the sounding sea.

ENGAGE

What type of mood is created by the first two lines?

What does it mean to love "with a love that was more than love"? Does the repetition make this line meaningless, or does it give it meaning?

At what point does the poem take a dark turn?

IMAGINE

What kind of soundtrack would go with this poem? What songs and sounds pair well with the story?

DEFINE

seraphs: *highest order of angels*

Coveted: *greatly desired*

sepulchre: *tomb*

dissever: *separate*

LENORE

Ah, broken is the golden bowl!—the spirit flown forever!
Let the bell toll!—a saintly soul floats on the **Stygian** river:—
And, **Guy De Vere**, hast *thou* no tear?—weep now or never more!
See! on yon drear and rigid **bier** low lies thy love, Lenore!
Come, let the burial rite be read—the funeral song be sung!—
An anthem for the queenliest dead that ever died so young—
A **dirge** for her the doubly dead in that she died so young.

"Wretches! ye loved her for her wealth and ye hated her for her pride;
And, when she fell in feeble health, ye blessed her—that she died:—
How *shall* the ritual, then, be read?—the **requiem** how be sung
By you—by yours, the evil eye—by yours the **slanderous** tongue
That did to death the innocence that died and died so young?"

Peccavimus!—yet rave not thus! but let a Sabbath song
Go up to God so solemnly the dead may feel no wrong!
The sweet Lenore hath gone before, with Hope that flew beside,
Leaving thee wild for the dear child that should have been thy bride—
For her, the fair and *debonair*, that now so lowly lies,
The life upon her yellow hair, but not within her eyes—
The life still there upon her hair; the death upon her eyes.

"**Avaunt**!—avaunt! to friends from fiends the **indignant** ghost is **riven**—
From Hell unto a high estate within the utmost Heaven—
From moan and groan to a golden throne beside the King of Heaven:—
Let *no* bell toll, then!—lest her soul, amid its hallowed **mirth**,
Should catch the note as it doth float up from the damned Earth!
And I—tonight my heart is light:—no dirge will I upraise,
But **waft** the angel on her flight with a **Pæan** of old days!"

Why might the speaker be so upset with Guy De Vere at the start of this poem?

In what other words or phrases do you notice the O and L sounds of the name Lenore?

Do you think Guy De Vere truly loved Lenore?

IMAGINE

If this poem were a question, what would it be asking? What's the answer?

DEFINE

Stygian: *River Styx in Hell*

Guy De Vere: *Lenore's intended husband*

bier: *coffin stand*

dirge: *mournful music*

requiem: *funeral hymn*

slanderous: *lying*

Peccavimus: *"we have sinned" (Latin)*

debonair: *stylish and charming*

Avaunt: *begone*

indignant: *angry*

riven: *torn apart*

mirth: *amusement*

waft: *move gently in the air*

Pæan: *song of praise*

Once upon a midnight dreary, while I pondered, weak and weary,
Over many a **quaint** and curious volume of forgotten lore—
While I nodded, nearly napping, suddenly there came a tapping,
As of some one gently rapping, rapping at my chamber door—
"'Tis some visitor," I muttered, "tapping at my chamber door—
        Only this, and nothing more."

Ah, distinctly I remember it was in the bleak December;
And each separate dying ember wrought its ghost upon the floor.
Eagerly I wished the morrow;—vainly I had sought to borrow
From my books **surcease** of sorrow—sorrow for the lost Lenore—
For the rare and radiant maiden whom the angels name Lenore—
        Nameless *here* for evermore.

And the silken, sad, uncertain rustling of each purple curtain
Thrilled me—filled me with fantastic terrors never felt before;
So that now, to still the beating of my heart, I stood repeating
" 'Tis some visitor **entreating** entrance at my chamber door—
Some late visitor entreating entrance at my chamber door;—
        This it is, and nothing more."

Presently my soul grew stronger; hesitating then no longer,
"Sir," said I, "or Madam, truly your forgiveness I **implore**;
But the fact is I was napping, and so gently you came rapping,
And so faintly you came tapping, tapping at my chamber door,
That I scarce was sure I heard you"—here I opened wide the door;—
        Darkness there and nothing more.

Deep into that darkness peering, long I stood there wondering, fearing,
Doubting, dreaming dreams no mortal ever dared to dream before;
But the silence was unbroken, and the stillness gave no **token**,
And the only word there spoken was the whispered word, "Lenore?"
This I whispered, and an echo murmured back the word, "Lenore!"
        Merely this and nothing more.

Back into the chamber turning, all my soul within me burning,
Soon again I heard a tapping somewhat louder than before.
"Surely," said I, "surely that is something at my window **lattice**;
Let me see, then, what **thereat** is, and this mystery explore—
Let my heart be still a moment and this mystery explore;—
      'Tis the wind and nothing more!"

Open here I flung the shutter, when, with many a flirt and flutter,
In there stepped a stately Raven of the saintly days of **yore**;
Not the least **obeisance** made he; not a minute stopped or stayed he;
But, with **mien** of lord or lady, perched above my chamber door—
Perched upon a bust of **Pallas** just above my chamber door—
      Perched, and sat, and nothing more.

ENGAGE

How is the mood set at the start of the poem?

Why do you think the raven only says one word?

Do you see any indications that all the events are a dream?

IMAGINE

Using stick figures, illustrate the beginning, middle, and end of this poem. How well does your three-image series work without the poem?

DEFINE

quaint: *unusual*

surcease: *pause*

entreating: *requesting*

implore: *beg*

token: *sign*

lattice: *crisscross frame*

thereat: *there*

yore: *long ago*

obeisance: *act of respect*

mien: *attitude*

Pallas: *Grecian goddess of wisdom*

ebony: *black*

beguiling:
fooling

fancy:
imagination

decorum:
behavior

countenance:
expression

crest: *tuft of
feathers on a bird's
head*

shorn: *cut off*

craven: *coward*

Plutonian:
underworld

Quoth: *said*

discourse:
speech

placid: *calm*

aptly:
appropriately

dirges: *mournful
songs*

betook: *started*

ungainly:
awkward

gaunt: *lean from
hunger*

Then this **ebony** bird **beguiling** my sad **fancy** into smiling,
By the grave and stern **decorum** of the **countenance** it wore.
"Though thy **crest** be **shorn** and shaven, thou," I said, "art sure no **craven**,
Ghastly grim and ancient Raven wandering from the Nightly shore—
Tell me what thy lordly name is on the Night's **Plutonian** shore!"
            Quoth the Raven "Nevermore."

Much I marvelled this ungainly fowl to hear **discourse** so plainly,
Though its answer little meaning—little relevancy bore;
For we cannot help agreeing that no living human being
Ever yet was blessed with seeing bird above his chamber door—
Bird or beast upon the sculptured bust above his chamber door,
            With such name as "Nevermore."

But the Raven, sitting lonely on the **placid** bust, spoke only
That one word, as if his soul in that one word he did outpour.
Nothing further then he uttered—not a feather then he fluttered—
Till I scarcely more than muttered, "Other friends have flown before—
On the morrow *he* will leave me, as my hopes have flown before."
            Then the bird said "Nevermore."

Startled at the stillness broken by reply so **aptly** spoken,
"Doubtless," said I, "what it utters is its only stock and store,
Caught from some unhappy master whom unmerciful Disaster
Followed fast and followed faster till his songs one burden bore—
Till the **dirges** of his Hope that melancholy burden bore
            Of 'Never—nevermore.' "

But the Raven still beguiling all my fancy into smiling,
Straight I wheeled a cushioned seat in front of bird, and bust and door;
Then upon the velvet sinking, I **betook** myself to linking
Fancy unto fancy, thinking what this ominous bird of yore—
What this grim, **ungainly**, ghastly, **gaunt** and ominous bird of yore
            Meant in croaking "Nevermore."

This I sat engaged in guessing, but no syllable expressing
To the fowl whose fiery eyes now burned into my bosom's core;
This and more I sat divining, with my head at ease reclining

On the cushion's velvet lining that the lamp-light gloated o'er,
But whose velvet violet lining with the lamp-light gloating o'er,
      She shall press, ah, nevermore!

Then methought the air grew denser, perfumed from an unseen **censer**
Swung by **seraphim** whose foot-falls tinkled on the tufted floor.
"Wretch," I cried, "thy God hath lent thee—by these angels he hath sent thee
Respite—respite and **nepenthe** from thy memories of Lenore;
Quaff, oh quaff this kind nepenthe and forget this lost Lenore!"
      Quoth the Raven "Nevermore."

"Prophet!" said I, "thing of evil!—prophet still, if bird or devil!
Whether Tempter sent, or whether tempest tossed thee here ashore,
Desolate yet all undaunted, on this desert land enchanted—
On this home by Horror haunted—tell me truly, I implore—
Is there—*is* there **balm in Gilead**?—tell me—tell me, I implore!"
      Quoth the Raven "Nevermore."

"Prophet!" said I, "thing of evil!—prophet still, if bird or devil!
By that Heaven that bends above us—by that God we both adore—
Tell this soul with sorrow laden if, within the distant **Aidenn**,
It shall clasp a sainted maiden whom the angels name Lenore—
Clasp a rare and radiant maiden whom the angels name Lenore."
      Quoth the Raven "Nevermore."

"Be that word our sign in parting, bird or fiend," I shrieked, **upstarting**—
"Get thee back into the tempest and the Night's Plutonian shore!
Leave no black plume as a token of that lie thy soul hath spoken!
Leave my loneliness unbroken!—**quit** the bust above my door!
Take thy beak from out my heart, and take thy form from off my door!"
      Quoth the Raven "Nevermore."

And the Raven, never flitting, still is sitting, *still* is sitting
On the pallid bust of Pallas just above my chamber door;
And his eyes have all the seeming of a demon's that is dreaming,
And the lamp-light o'er him streaming throws his shadow on the floor;
And my soul from out that shadow that lies floating on the floor
      Shall be lifted—nevermore!

censer: *bowl for burning incense*

seraphim: *highest order of angels*

Respite: *moment of relief*

nepenthe: *in Homer's* Odyssey, *a drug that stops grief*

Quaff: *drink*

balm in Gilead: *a Biblical question about the lack of healing in the region of Gilead*

Aidenn: *paradise (Arabic)*

upstarting: *jumping up in surprise*

quit: *leave*

THE LAKE—TO—

In spring of youth it was my lot
To haunt of the wide world a spot
The which I could not love the less—
So lovely was the loneliness
Of a wild lake, with black rock bound,
And the tall pines that towered around.

But when the Night had thrown her **pall**
Upon that spot, as upon all,
And the mystic wind went by
Murmuring in melody—
Then—ah then I would awake
To the terror of the lone lake.

Yet that terror was not fright,
But a tremulous delight—
A feeling not the jewelled mine
Could teach or bribe me to define—
Nor Love—although the Love were thine.

Death was in that poisonous wave,
And in its **gulf** a fitting grave
For him who **thence** could **solace** bring
To his lone imagining
Whose solitary soul could make
An **Eden** of that dim lake.

ENGAGE

As a youth, why did the speaker find the lake so appealing?

Why might the "poisonous waves" be a "fitting grave"? For whom or what?

Why do you think there are so many contrasting ideas here?

IMAGINE

Sometimes a poem is a window. Looking through the window of this poem, what do you see?

DEFINE

pall: *coffin covering*

gulf: *depth*

thence: *consequently*

solace: *comfort*

Eden: *unspoiled paradise*

PART III

The World Fantastic

THE BELLS

1.

Hear the sledges with the bells—
Silver bells!
What a world of merriment their melody foretells!
How they tinkle, tinkle, tinkle,
In the icy air of night!
While the stars that oversprinkle
All the heavens, seem to twinkle
With a crystalline delight;
Keeping time, time, time,
In a sort of **Runic rhyme**,
To the **tintinnabulation** that so musically wells
From the bells, bells, bells, bells,
Bells, bells, bells—
From the jingling and the tinkling of the bells.

2.

Hear the mellow wedding bells
Golden bells!
What a world of happiness their harmony foretells!
Through the balmy air of night
How they ring out their delight!—
From the molten-golden notes,
And all in tune,
What a liquid **ditty** floats
To the turtle-dove that listens, while she gloats
On the moon!
Oh, from out the sounding cells,
What a gush of **euphony voluminously wells**!
How it swells!
How it dwells
On the Future! how it tells
Of the rapture that **impels**
To the swinging and the ringing
Of the bells, bells, bells!—
Of the bells, bells, bells, bells,
Bells, bells, bells—
To the rhyming and the chiming of the bells!

⚙ ENGAGE

How might the repeated words in this poem be like the clanging of bells?

Why do you think the stanzas grow in length through the poem?

How might this be a poem about madness?

💡 IMAGINE

Replace the lyrics of a song you know well with this poem. How well does this new version work?

🔤 DEFINE

Runic rhyme: *magic spell*

tintinnabulation: *ringing sound*

ditty: *simple song*

euphony voluminously wells: *pleasant sounds rising*

impels: *urges*

alarum: *alarm*

turbulency: *state of agitation*

expostulation: *strong disapproval*

palpitating: *trembling*

clangor: *continuous loud ringing*

monody: *music with only one melodic line*

Ghouls: *evil spirits*

Pæan: *song of praise*

knells: *ring solemnly*

3.

Hear the loud **alarum** bells—

Brazen bells!

What tale of terror, now, their **turbulency** tells!

In the startled ear of night

How they scream out their affright!

Too much horrified to speak,

They can only shriek, shriek,

Out of tune,

In a clamorous appealing to the mercy of the fire—

In a mad **expostulation** with the deaf and frantic fire,

Leaping higher, higher, higher,

With a desperate desire,

And a resolute endeavor

Now—now to sit or never,

By the side of the pale-faced moon.

Oh, the bells, bells, bells!

What a tale their terror tells

Of Despair!

How they clang, and clash, and roar!
What a horror they outpour
In the bosom of the **palpitating** air!
Yet the ear, it fully knows,
By the twanging,
And the clanging,
How the danger ebbs and flows:—
Yes, the ear distinctly tells,

In the jangling,
And the wrangling,
How the danger sinks and swells,
By the sinking or the swelling in the anger of the bells—
Of the bells—
Of the bells, bells, bells, bells,
Bells, bells, bells—
In the clamor and the **clangor** of the bells!

4.
Hear the tolling of the bells—
Iron bells !
What a world of solemn thought their **monody** compels!
In the silence of the night,
How we shiver with affright
At the melancholy meaning of their tone!
For every sound that floats
From the rust within their throats
Is a groan.
And the people—ah, the people—
They that dwell up in the steeple,
All alone,
And who, tolling, tolling, tolling,
In that muffled monotone,
Feel a glory in so rolling
On the human heart a stone—
They are neither man nor woman—
They are neither brute nor human,
They are **Ghouls**:—
And their king it is who tolls:—
And he rolls, rolls, rolls, rolls,
A **Pæan** from the bells!
And his merry bosom swells
With the Pæan of the bells!
And he dances, and he yells;

Keeping time, time, time,
In a sort of Runic rhyme,
To the Pæan of the bells—
Of the bells:
Keeping time, time, time,
In a sort of Runic rhyme,
To the throbbing of the bells—
Of the bells, bells, bells—
To the sobbing of the bells:—
Keeping time, time, time,
As he **knells**, knells, knells,
In a happy Runic rhyme,
To the rolling of the bells—
Of the bells, bells, bells:—
To the tolling of the bells—
Of the bells, bells, bells, bells,
Bells, bells, bells—
To the moaning and the groaning of the bells.

THE HAUNTED PALACE

In the greenest of our valleys
    By good angels **tenanted**,
Once a fair and stately palace—
    Radiant palace—reared its head.
In the monarch Thought's dominion—
    It stood there!
Never **seraph** spread a **pinion**
    Over fabric half so fair!

Banners yellow, glorious, golden,
    On its roof did float and flow—
(This—all this—was in the olden
    Time long ago)
And every gentle air that **dallied**,
    In that sweet day,
Along the **ramparts** plumed and **pallid**,
    A winged odor went away.

Wanderers in that happy valley,
    Through two **luminous** windows, saw
Spirits moving musically
    To a lute's well-tuned law,
Round about a throne where, sitting,
    Porphyrogene!
In state his glory well befitting,
    The ruler of the realm was seen.

And all with pearl and ruby glowing
    Was the fair palace door,
Through which came flowing, flowing, flowing,
    And sparkling evermore,
A troop of **Echoes**, whose sweet duty
    Was but to sing,
In voices of surpassing beauty,
    The wit and wisdom of their king.

But evil things, in robes of sorrow,
    Assailed the monarch's high estate;
(Ah, let us mourn!—for never **morrow**
    Shall dawn upon him, desolate!)
And round about his home the glory
    That blushed and bloomed,
Is but a dim-remembered story
    Of the old-time entombed.

And travellers, now, within that valley,
    Through the **encrimsoned** windows see
Vast forms that move fantastically
    To a **discordant** melody;
While, like a ghastly rapid river,
    Through the pale door
A hideous **throng** rush out forever
    And laugh—but smile no more.

ENGAGE

What might the haunted palace represent?

Where do you notice hyperbole (purposeful overstatement)?

What do people now see when they travel past the haunted palace?

IMAGINE

How might you adapt this poem into a graphic novel? What would you need to add, subtract, or change?

DEFINE

tenanted: *occupied*

seraph: *highest order of angels*

pinion: *wing*

dallied: *played*

ramparts: *defensive walls*

pallid: *pale*

luminous: *full of light*

Porphyrogene: *person born into royalty*

Echoes: *spirits*

Assailed: *attacked*

morrow: *tomorrow*

encrimsoned: *dyed red*

discordant: *harsh sounding*

throng: *crowd*

*Why might this poem
start with a farewell
kiss?*

*Why do you think
this poem takes place
on a "surf-tormented
shore"?*

*How do you see the
speaker's attitude
changing in this poem?*

IMAGINE

*What character from a
movie or TV show does
this speaker remind you
of?*

DEFINE

avow: *openly confess*

A DREAM WITHIN
A DREAM

Take this kiss upon the brow!
And, in parting from you now,
Thus much let me **avow**—
You are not wrong, who deem
That my days have been a dream;
Yet if hope has flown away
In a night, or in a day,
In a vision, or in none,
Is it therefore the less *gone*?
All that we see or seem
Is but a dream within a dream.

I stand amid the roar
Of a surf-tormented shore,
And I hold within my hand
Grains of the golden sand—
How few! yet how they creep
Through my fingers to the deep,
While I weep—while I weep!
O God! can I not grasp
Them with a tighter clasp?
O God! can I not save
One from the pitiless wave?
Is *all* that we see or seem
But a dream within a dream?

ELDORADO

Gaily bedight,
A **gallant** knight,
In sunshine and in shadow,
Had journeyed long,
Singing a song,
In search of Eldorado.

But he grew old—
This knight so bold—
And o'er his heart a shadow
Fell, as he found
No spot of ground
That looked like Eldorado.

And, as his strength
Failed him at length,
He met a **pilgrim** shadow—
"Shadow," said he,
"Where can it be—
This land of Eldorado?"

"Over the Mountains
Of the Moon,
Down the Valley of the Shadow,
Ride, boldly ride,"
The shade replied,—
"If you seek for Eldorado!"

ENGAGE

Why do you think there's so much darkness and shadow in this poem?

What might Eldorado represent other than a lost city of untold riches?

Is the pursuit of Eldorado a foolish one?

IMAGINE

If this poem were written today, what would Eldorado be? And where would people search for it?

DEFINE

Eldorado: *legendary city of gold*

Gaily: *colorfully*

bedight: *dressed*

gallant: *heroic*

pilgrim: *person on a religious journey*

DREAM-LAND

By a route obscure and lonely,
Haunted by ill angels only,
Where an **Eidolon**, named Night,
On a black throne reigns upright,
I have reached these lands but newly
From an ultimate dim **Thule**—
From a wild weird **clime** that **lieth**, **sublime**,
  Out of Space—out of Time.

Bottomless **vales** and boundless floods,
And chasms, and caves, and **Titan** woods,
With forms that no man can discover
For the dews that drip all over;
Mountains toppling evermore
Into seas without a shore;
Seas that restlessly aspire,
Surging, unto skies of fire;
Lakes that endlessly outspread
Their lone waters—lone and dead,—
Their still waters—still and chilly
With the snows of the **lolling** lily.

By the lakes that thus outspread
Their lone waters, lone and dead,—
Their sad waters, sad and chilly
With the snows of the lolling lily,—
By the mountains—near the river
Murmuring lowly, murmuring ever,—
By the grey woods,—by the swamp
Where the toad and the newt encamp,—
By the dismal **tarns** and pools
  Where dwell the **Ghouls**,—
By each spot the most unholy—
In each nook most melancholy,—
There the traveller meets **aghast**
Sheeted Memories of the Past—
Shrouded forms that start and sigh
As they pass the wanderer by—
White-robed forms of friends long given,
In agony, to the Earth—and Heaven.

For the heart whose woes are **legion**
'Tis a peaceful, soothing region—
For the spirit that walks in shadow
O! it is an **Eldorado**!
But the traveller, travelling through it,
May not—dare not openly view it;
Never its mysteries are exposed
To the weak human eye unclosed;
So wills its King, who hath forbid
The uplifting of the fringed lid;
And thus the sad Soul that here passes
Beholds it but through darkened glasses.

By a route **obscure** and lonely,
Haunted by ill angels only,
Where an Eidolon, named Night,
On a black throne reigns upright,
I have wandered home but newly
From this ultimate dim Thule.

⚙ ENGAGE

Why do you think no other human visitors are on this "obscure and lonely" route?

What's the effect of so much repetition in this poem?

In what way is this strange place an Eldorado?

💡 IMAGINE

How do you imagine the King will respond to this poet intruder?

🅰 DEFINE

Eidolon: *phantom*

Thule: *northernmost part of the habitable ancient world*

clime: *climate*

lieth: *lie*

sublime: *supreme excellence*

vales: *valleys*

Titan: *giants from Greek myth*

lolling: *hanging loosely*

tarns: *small mountain lake*

Ghouls: *evil spirits*

aghast: *with shock*

legion: *vast number*

Eldorado: *legendary city of gold*

obscure: *concealed*

ENGAGE

Does the moon's light always overpower the stars?

Why do you think the "distant fire" is so appealing to the speaker?

Other than a celestial body, what might the Evening Star represent?

IMAGINE

How would this poem change if it were set on the moon? Or another planet? Or in a spaceship?

DEFINE

noontide: *noon*

shroud: *burial cloth*

EVENING STAR

'Twas **noontide** of summer,
 And mid-time of night;
And stars, in their orbits,
 Shone pale, thro' the light
Of the brighter, cold moon,
 'Mid planets her slaves,
Herself in the Heavens,
 Her beam on the waves.
 I gaz'd awhile
 On her cold smile;
Too cold—too cold for me—
 There pass'd, as a **shroud**,
 A fleecy cloud,
And I turn'd away to thee,
 Proud Evening Star,
 In thy glory afar,
And dearer thy beam shall be;
 For joy to my heart
 Is the proud part
Thou bearest in Heav'n at night,
 And more I admire
 Thy distant fire,
Than that colder, lowly light.

SONNET—TO SCIENCE

Science! true daughter of Old Time thou art!
    Who **alterest** all things with thy peering eyes.
Why preyest thou thus upon the poet's heart,
    Vulture, whose wings are dull realities?
How should he love thee? or how deem thee wise,
    Who wouldst not leave him in his wandering
To seek for treasure in the jewelled skies
    Albeit he soared with an undaunted wing?
Hast thou not dragged **Diana** from her **car**?
    And driven the **Hamadryad** from the wood
To seek a shelter in some happier star?
    Hast thou not torn the **Naiad** from her flood,
The Elfin from the green grass, and from me
    The summer dream beneath the **tamarind** tree?

⚡ IMAGINE

How might science respond to this in a poem entitled "Sonnet—To Nature"?

🔤 DEFINE

alterest: *changes*

Diana: *Roman goddess of the hunt*

car: *chariot*

Hamadryad: *tree spirit*

Naiad: *water spirit*

tamarind: *fruit-bearing shade tree*

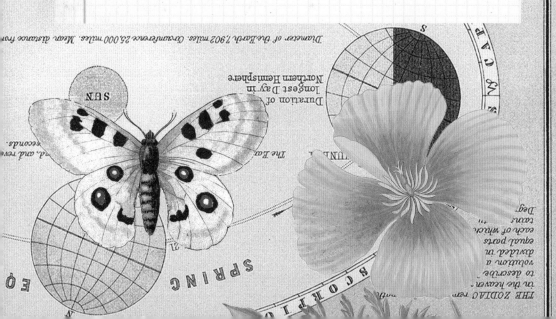

SERENADE

So sweet the hour—so calm the time,
I feel it more than half a crime,
When Nature sleeps and stars are mute,
To **mar** the silence ev'n with **lute**.
At rest on ocean's brilliant dyes
An image of **Elysium** lies:
Seven **Pleiades** entranced in Heaven
Form in the deep another seven:
Endymion nodding from above
Sees in the sea a second love:
Within the valleys dim and brown,
And on the spectral mountain's crown
The wearied light is lying down:
And earth, and stars, and sea, and sky
Are **redolent** of sleep, as I
Am redolent of thee and thine
Enthralling love, my **Adeline**.
But **list**, O list!—so soft and low
Thy lover's voice tonight shall flow
That, scarce awake, thy soul shall deem
My words the music of a dream.
Thus, while no single sound too rude,
Upon thy slumber shall intrude,
Our thoughts, our souls—O God above!
In every deed shall mingle, love.

ENGAGE

What do you think it means for stars to be mute?

Why is this poem set beside the ocean?

In what way is this poem a serenade? (A serenade is music played outdoors to a beloved person.)

IMAGINE

How would this poem be changed if Adeline loves someone else? Or if Adeline is deceased? Or if Adeline isn't actually a person?

DEFINE

mar: *spoil*

lute: *small stringed instrument*

Elysium: *place of perfect happiness in Greek myth*

Pleiades: *bright star cluster in the constellation Taurus*

Endymion: *beautiful young man beloved by the moon in Greek myth*

redolent: *fragrant*

Adeline: *name meaning "of noble birth"*

list: *listen*

Ten Things to Know About Edgar Allan Poe

1   Edgar Allan Poe (1809–1849) is best-known for writing spooky stories, though his original intention was to become a famous poet.

2   In addition to writing poems and tales of terror, Poe wrote science fiction, detective stories, and satires. He was also one of the most important literary critics of his time.

3   His parents died when he was still a toddler, and he was taken in—but never adopted—by the wealthy but miserly John Allan.

4   While he's known today as "Edgar Allan Poe," he became estranged from his foster family and nearly always signed his name "Edgar A. Poe."

5   He adored many women, but he married only one—his first cousin Virginia Clemm. When they married, she was 13 and he was 27.

6   Despite the wild popularity of his poem "The Raven," it probably only earned him about $10.

7   The circumstances of his death were odd—he was found semi-conscious in a Baltimore tavern and died days later. Some believe that he had rabies, while others believe he suffered from a neurological disorder.

8   He wrote that poetry is the "rhythmical creation of beauty" and that "melancholy" is the most appropriate poetic tone.

9   Most of his famous poems are about death, beautiful women, or the death of a beautiful woman.

10 Though he produced fewer than 100 poems, his approach to crafting poems syllable by syllable and sound by sound led him to write some of the most readable and memorable poems ever.

Commentary on the Poems

PART I: LOVE & LONGING

"To Zante"

The speaker appreciates the beauty of the island of Zante, and it brings about the memory of a lost love (likely Edgar's first fiancée, Elmira Shelton).

NOTICE HOW THE SPEAKER LINKS THE ISLAND'S BEAUTY WITH LOST LOVE, WHICH MAKES IT CURSED GROUND.

"Alone"

In realizing they're different from others, the speaker feels alone in a sense of loneliness that feels as powerful as a demon.

NOTICE HOW POWERFULLY POE FELT ABOUT BEING DIFFERENT FROM OTHER PEOPLE, SINGLED OUT, CHOSEN, OR EVEN CURSED.

"A Valentine"

This love poem teases readers with a riddle that can be solved using clues in the lines.

NOTICE HOW SOLVING THE RIDDLE REQUIRES FINDING A WOMAN'S NAME (FRANCES SARGENT OSGOOD—A POPULAR FEMALE POET) BY READING THE FIRST LETTER OF LINE ONE, THE SECOND LETTER OF LINE TWO, ETC.

"To Helen"

Written in response to the death of a childhood friend's mother, this poem celebrates her beauty as legendary. Her loveliness transports the speaker into the realm of Greek myths.

NOTICE HOW THE POEM USES HELEN (CONNECTING HER TO HELEN OF TROY, THE MOST BEAUTIFUL WOMAN IN THE ANCIENT WORLD) INSTEAD OF THE ACTUAL NAME OF THE DECEASED (JANE).

"To M—"

In somewhat scandalous language for the time, the speaker reveals deep affection for a lady.

NOTICE HOW THIS WAS WRITTEN BY A VERY YOUNG EDGAR (ONLY 20 AT THE TIME), SO THE "YEARS OF LOVE" IS CLEARLY AN EXAGGERATION.

"The Happiest Day"

The speaker is getting over a broken heart, and the beloved (likely Elmira Shelton from "To Zante") has someone new.

NOTICE HOW THE SPEAKER WOULDN'T CHOOSE TO RELIVE PAST HAPPY MOMENTS—THE COST IS TOO HIGH.

"For Annie"

The speaker is unmoving in bed, so sick as to be mistaken for dead, though dreams of Annie—a dear friend—are soothing and healing.

NOTICE HOW THE SPEAKER REFERS TO LIFE AS A DISEASE.

"To One in Paradise"

The speaker experiences a deep sadness over the loss of a beloved person. The only thing that eases the pain is the peace offered by "nightly dreams."

NOTICE HOW THE BELOVED HAS AN EVERLASTING PRESENCE IN THE SPEAKER'S LIFE, DESPITE BEING DEAD.

"Romance"

Romance is a sleepy bird that taught the speaker joy as a child; but as an adult, life's hardships leave little time for beauty.

NOTICE HOW THE IDEA OF A BIRD SPEAKING HERE (TEACHING THE ALPHABET) CONNECTS WITH THE TALKING BIRD IN "THE RAVEN."

PART II: THE GREAT BEYOND

"The Conqueror Worm"

In this pessimistic poem, an audience of angels watch a tragic play called "Man," where the hero is the "Conqueror Worm" (Death).

NOTICE HOW THE ANGELS WATCH BUT CAN'T HELP FACELESS PEOPLE SUFFERING ON STAGE.

"The City in the Sea"

This dark, brooding poem—a companion piece to "The Valley of Unrest"—depicts a city that sinks to the bottom of the sea.

NOTICE HOW THIS COLD, DEAD CITY CONTRASTS WITH THE LIVELY, MYSTICAL CITY OF ATLANTIS, WHICH ALSO VANISHED BENEATH THE WAVES.

"The Valley of Unrest"

This companion piece to "The City in the Sea" shows how a once-happy valley has changed after people "had gone unto the wars."

NOTICE HOW THE VALLEY CHANGES FROM A STATE OF MOURNING TO RESTLESSNESS AND MOTION.

"Spirits of the Dead"

Embracing beauty more than sadness, this poem considers the greatest "mystery of mysteries," which is moving from this life into the next.

NOTICE HOW THE SPEAKER'S MOOD CHANGES— IT STARTS WITH SADNESS, THEN MOVES TO ANGER, AND ENDS IN ACCEPTANCE.

"Annabel Lee"

A child whose love for another was so special that angels killed the beloved out of jealousy. Years later, the speaker sleeps beside the body of Annabel Lee in her tomb by the sea.

NOTICE HOW RHYTHM AND REPETITION CREATE A POWERFUL READ-ALOUD QUALITY.

"Lenore"

This poem offers a conversation between a judgmental mourner and the fiancé (Guy De Vere) of the beautiful Lenore. De Vere refuses to mourn her since her soul now sits next to God.

NOTICE HOW BEAUTY AND DEATH ARE WOVEN SO DEEPLY INTO THIS POEM.

"The Raven"

In this popular poem, a mourning speaker is disturbed by a raven that torments him with a single repeated word: "Nevermore."

NOTICE HOW THE RAVEN SYMBOLIZES THE LOSS THAT THE SPEAKER HAS SUFFERED.

"The Lake—To—"

As a youth, the speaker spent a lot of time near a lake which was terrifying and yet beautiful and delightful.

NOTICE HOW THE SPEAKER IS GRIEVING A LOSS ("NIGHT HAD THROWN HER PALL / UPON THAT SPOT").

PART III: THE WORLD FANTASTIC

"The Bells"
The speaker has increasingly harsh reactions to four different types of bells—the light, happy sounds of sleigh bells and wedding bells, and the clanging of heavier iron bells like those that warn of public emergencies or are used at funerals.

NOTICE HOW THERE'S NO SET RHYME PATTERN, THOUGH THE POEM USES LOTS OF RHYME AND CAREFUL RHYTHMIC CHOICES.

"The Haunted Palace"
Travelers used to hear music and see dancing spirits when they passed the wonderful palace, but "evil things" took over, so the former beauty of the palace and its king are long gone.

NOTICE HOW THE IMAGE OF A DECAYING MANSION CAN BE SEEN AS A METAPHOR FOR INSANITY. THIS POEM WAS REFERENCED AND EXPLAINED BY RODERICK USHER IN THE SHORT STORY "THE FALL OF THE HOUSE OF USHER."

"A Dream Within a Dream"
After a goodbye kiss with a beloved person, the speaker wonders if their time together was merely a dream, since it flew by so swiftly. That leads to a larger concern—is all of life an illusion, a mere "dream within a dream"?

NOTICE HOW THE FIRST STANZA SHOWS HOPE, WHEREAS THE SECOND STANZA SHOWS THE SPEAKER IN DESPAIR.

"Eldorado"
Published in 1849 (right around the Gold Rush in America), this poem shares how a "gallant knight" spends his entire life seeking the lost city of gold without finding it.

NOTICE HOW THE SHADE TELLS THE SPEAKER—WHO IS NEAR DEATH—TO "RIDE, BOLDLY RIDE" AHEAD, SUGGESTING THAT ELDORADO IS FOUND ONLY IN DEATH.

"Dream-Land"
This poem details the speaker's experiences in a cold, strange world that's haunted by ghosts.

NOTICE HOW THIS LANDSCAPE IS ABSENT OF COLORS—THERE'S ONLY WHITE, GRAY, AND BLACK.

"Evening Star"
While looking up at the heavens, the speaker turns away from the coldly beautiful moon to admire the "distant fire" of the evening star.

NOTICE HOW BOTH CELESTIAL BODIES CAN BE SEEN AS TWO VERY DIFFERENT TYPES OF WOMEN IN THE SPEAKER'S LIFE.

"Sonnet—To Science"
The speaker sees science as a way of looking at the world that denies or destroys imagination.

NOTICE HOW SCIENCE IS PRESENTED AS A HOSTILE FORCE—A "VULTURE" THAT PREYS UPON A "POET'S HEART."

"Serenade"

The speaker's nighttime view of the ocean inspires an appreciation for the beauty of nature and silence. In this wonder-filled moment, the speaker quietly ("so soft and low") speaks to a beloved, such that she "shall deem / My words the music of a dream."

NOTICE HOW MULTIPLE REFERENCES TO CELESTIAL BODIES AND GREEK MYTHOLOGY GIVE THE SPEAKER'S LOVE A LARGER-THAN-LIFE QUALITY.

To Learn More About Edgar Allan Poe

1 *A Raven Named Grip: How a Bird Inspired Two Famous Writers, Charles Dickens and Edgar Allan Poe* by Marilyn Singer. Dial Books, 2021.

2 *Who Was Edgar Allan Poe?* by Jim Gigliotti. Penguin Workshop, 2015.

Bibliography

1 *Collected Works of Edgar Allan Poe, Volume 1: Poems.* Edited by Thomas Olive Mabbott. Harvard University Press, 1969.

2 The Edgar Allan Poe Society of Baltimore. www.eapoe.org

Special thanks to Dr. Scott Peeples (College of Charleston) for reviewing this manuscript.